staying

in

D1555024

love

Poetry by

Julia Fehrenbacher

To Kristen –
Happy 55th Birthday
to you! Here is
to becoming
more & more
of who you
are.

Wishing you
an abundance
of Love. Always.
Happy 55th!

With an
abundance
of Love –
Julia

CCB Publishing
British Columbia, Canada

Staying in Love

Library and Archives Canada Cataloguing in Publication
Title: Staying in love / poetry by Julia Fehrenbacher.
Names: Fehrenbacher, Julia, 1970-, author.
Issued in print and electronic formats.
Identifiers: ISBN 9781771435024 (pbk) | ISBN 9781771435031 (pdf)
Additional cataloguing data available from Library and Archives Canada

Front cover and interior images © Julia Fehrenbacher

Publisher: CCB Publishing
            British Columbia, Canada
            www.ccbpublishing.com

For my Aunt Maye, and the many others, who left us far too soon.

For my beloved daughters, Marielle and Lily, who have grown my heart a thousand times its original size. And to girls and women everywhere, the world so needs the gifts that only you have—please, don't ever be quiet.

For my husband, Matt, and the many beautiful others who continue to nudge me back to my bigness.

For my mom and dad who love and support me no matter what.

dear you,

I write to you from my front porch on an absolutely gorgeous, sunshiny spring day. Two crows are sailing in circles above my head, the cherry tree across the street is in full blossoming beauty, the surrounding oaks are swollen with buds, soon to be a leafy wonder, neighbors are strolling by with dogs and children, daffodils are celebrating their own flowering. The breeze is sweet and subtle and just right.

It is hard to believe from my spot in the sunshine that our world is in crisis.

But, *my gosh*. What a time it is. A global pandemic unlike anything any of us have ever experienced, tremendous political and social unrest, devastating wildfires, people desperately seeking refuge (inside and outside of themselves), a planet in dire need of our full and immediate attention.

And still, even when, even now—*there is so much beauty*.

When one storm after another blows us to the ground, how do we not stay on our knees, throw in the dirty towel, curse it all, write off everyone who disagrees with us, fall forever into despair? How do we continue to show up for our loved ones, strangers, our glorious planet, ourselves?

The question I want to ask is: *How can we not?*

Now, more than ever, we must show up with our best selves, we must become (or continue to be) part of the healing, rather than adding to the hurt. It is critical.

Everything truly depends on our rising, on our digging beneath the layers of our small, fearful selves, to the bigness that each and every one of us has inside. Everything depends on our resolve to stay and stay in love.

In my poem, *Hold Out Your Hand*, I write:

Stop asking: Am I good enough?
Ask only: Am I showing up with love?

Yes, I think this is the question to ask.

My deep hope is that the poems that fill these pages act as both a gentle and fierce nudge. A nudge back to love, to stillness, to remembering your inherent worth, to staying in love with this ugly, tired, sick, wild, beautiful mess of a world. Even when. Even when. Even when.

♡ Julia

*What I really need is to drink a glass of
water slowly, because there is enough—
there is enough fast in this world.
And every real thing is found inside the
soft arms of a moment.*

*And because, in the midst of so much
trauma and terror, it is vital to bow to
such holy, ordinary things.*

Contents

s t a y i n g

Return, whispers the moment.

I am right here.

living awake

It begins with an ache, a deep-belly
breath, a cup of hot tea on the sun-soaked deck.

It begins with a prayer said aloud
to the empty kitchen, space enough to hear
the want beneath the want beneath the want.

It begins with a thank you
for what is, a remembering that all
of it is temporary, none of it guaranteed,
every last bit of it precious.

It begins with slowing to the pace of silence,
then getting closer, closer
than you have ever gotten before. Then even
a little bit closer. To breath, river, heartache,
sunlight. Because, as Yeats said:

*The world is full of magical things patiently
waiting for our senses to grow sharper.*

It begins, always, with a moment fully allowed.

It begins over and over and over again, new, every day—
with the courage to persist, to do it differently, to walk
the way only you can walk. The courage
to stand all the way up for what holds
and heals, to fiercely declare that enough
is enough—no more excuses, no more holding in
or back, no more pretending
to be small, damn it. Because you are not
small. You have never, ever been small.

And God, how this sleeping world needs your bigness.

It begins with picking up the light
and dancing with it all night long, vowing
to never put it down. And then scattering
it like seed to every hurting heart.

It begins with a thank you for what is,
a remembering that all
of it is temporary, none of it guaranteed—

every last bit of it precious.

hold out your hand

Let's forget the world for a while
fall back and back
into the hush and holy
of now

are you listening? This breath
invites you
to write the first word
of your new story

your new story begins with this:

You matter.

You are needed—empty
and naked
willing to say yes
and yes and yes.

Do you see
the sun shines, day after day
whether you have faith
or not, sparrows continue
to sing their song
even when you forget to sing
yours.

Stop asking: *Am I good enough?*
Ask only: *Am I showing up with love?*

Life is not a straight line
it's a downpour of gifts, please—
hold out your hand

she is speaking

Do you hear her under there?
She is speaking.

Her voice quieter, fiercer, more certain
than the others. Her whispers
will make little sense to your sensible mind.

Listen anyway.

This morning I stood still. So still for so long
that I saw shadow slip slide drift
her way across leaf-strewn lawn.

And, I know. Not because of a thought,
not because I have been told or taught,
not because I have read it in a hundred
wise books, I know
that stillness is the way to her.

And that we are sick and dying
from listening to the cowardly voices of others.

Inside, underneath, in-between the senseless
hurry, she is here. Like sunshine,
like always-shifting shadow, like the lilies
in the light-filled field—she
is speaking.

Will you bend closer to listen? Will you follow
her quiet roar? Can you think of a single thing
that matters more?

instructions for today (part I)

Try this:

Close your tired eyes, breathe
deeply. Say thank you. Even if
you're poor or sick
or without hope

let shouts
and whispers speak
until the hard
and stern
fade

into a watery ripple
of love.

instructions for today (part II)

Sit and listen to a tree for longer
than feels appropriate. Close eyes
until the hurting demands
settle, until only the invisible speaks.

Ask yourself the same questions
you've been asking
everyone else. Be still
until you hear
the answers. Trust me—
they will come.

Tell the truth. The one that has simmered
and boiled inside you. It is yours.
No one can shape it
or take it. When words fall out
notice how sure and steady
your feet feel on the ground—it is meant
to be this way.

Remember, there is no promise
of tomorrow. Let this truth
live inside you until you can't help
but turn toward love.

You are not a victim. You
are a truth-telling warrior
who gets up again
and again and again. Who stands
in the middle of the mess
and says:

I don't know, but I'm ready to listen.

Then open
your eyes
and head on home.

even this

There are many reasons to say no. No, not
this. Oh please, not that. Not this sink
full of last night's dishes, not Monday again, not
the demands demands demands,
not the grief, the sorrow, that swallows the ground.

But, please, I say to the moment, let me stay.

Let me greet even this with open hand,
loosened heart, as if
the perfect teacher has arrived
at my door knocking.

Come in, I'd say, as kettle whistles
its welcome. Sit. Stay.

Stay for as long as you need to.

Please, I say to today, please
make these eyes new again. Let me place feet
on morning ground and say *thank you*, let
me remember this breath I breathe
is *Life*—that every sip, every
slip, every step, every single
smudge of hard has been for
me. Please,

I say to the moment, let me be swept
off my feet with amazement that the tiny seeds
I scattered so hopefully last fall
have turned into dancing red poppies.

Thank you, I say to rising sun, for even
the hardest things, that show me how strong
these branches, how deep these roots—

how to turn tiny seeds
into dazzling red poppies.

Please, I say to the pen, let me follow
you into the new, the never before,

not because of where you will take me,
but because you set me down in the center
of this living, leave me unleashed,
untucked, unsaddled—

shirttails dancing in the wind.

choose again

This is the time
to be here in this body
to weave words
with this heart, these hands
to let

this voice say
what it came here to say

this is the time to open eyes, to plant
feet on this ground
to feel the undeniable holy
in each blink, each breath

feathered friend on old, weathered
fence, wild iris breathing
into blossom, branches drenched
in sunlight

God is too small
a word for all this miracle—too small
for the sky of stars
in these limbs and lungs.

This is the time
to choose again, to hold out hand
and heart—to leave
the shade of mind
to let life fall
fall in

there is no there

Have you looked around today?

I don't mean in a hurried way or
in a trying way. I mean really
looked.

Inhaled. Leaned in. Got close enough to smell
to taste—to see. To listen. Maybe even
to touch.

You run so fast. So worried, so harried—
should
must
faster
never enough
gotta get there gotta get there gotta get there.

Do you see the tiny crocus all bathed in white, daffodil
just about to bloom? Sky resting silently
above your troubled head?

Could you stop
and breathe? Let sun shine
in. Could you consider
that there is no there? There is no
there.

Only here. Only here. Only here.

Could you bow to the nearest tree? She has infinite
secrets to share. Need you look further than her holy
branches, her humble roots?

Everything is calling to you. To you. *Yes—you.*

Everything is oozing God (which is really just a word for everything and is far too small a word to hold everything, which excludes nothing. No one).

Are you listening?

It all speaks. It all speaks right now. Whispers answers to your every question. I'll ask you again—
are you listening?

she who watches

It appears to be the end again.

The end of another season, another
day. Blackberries juiceless and drying
on their vines, crickets and restless leaves
grace the air with a song
only they, only they can sing.

In the distance, a tired train whistles.

Evening light gathers—
gathers every listening thing
in her warm, safe arms.

A moment disguised as ordinary,
all tangled up and dripping
in miracle.

She, the watcher of it all—

the one who rests beneath, beneath the noise
and need, the empty-armed one who sits
cross-legged and still, opening,
opening to all of it just as it is, opening
to a moment that has already written itself.

refuge

She decides to sit still until the dust of the day
settles, until she drops

below
beyond
beneath

the layers of hard and heavy. Until she hears
the true things that stillness speaks, things like—

it is enough to be you.

She decides to sit still until enoughness seeps
into blood bones breath, until the pull
to do more, be more, fades
like evening's softening sun, until she
remembers that

below
beyond
beneath

all that has been added
is the true—
the very truest thing.

advice from an oak

From her rooted spot in the sunlight,
oak whispers the familiar words:
Start where you are.

So, I do.

I start here with steaming mint tea, rhododendrons
blooming pink, this always-fear of the loud, blank
page—with the worry that, perhaps,
I can't make any of it beautiful.

I'll start with the whole wobbly
mess of me, with the stubborn feeling
that I am missing the thing
I am supposed to find
and I don't know why or what's next
or how much time.

I'll start here by listening
to this deep and beneath voice,
the one that aches and asks
and asks and aches to be all the way allowed,
all the way heard. Here with quiet, blank
page that opens wide to each finally-freed word.

I'll start by inviting you to your own
blank page, by daring you to allow
the whole wobbly mess to tumble finally-free

until every last crumb of a thing
crawls, curves, bows its stubborn way
to beautiful.

one breath away

There is something about this evening's
walk. Maybe it's the way sunshine fills all
the little puddles, or the wide-awake green
of the farmer's field. Or maybe it's the soft,
end-of-another-day sky

I don't know. Though I think
it has more to do with how here
I am, how open these eyes, how listening
these ears. Each step carries body closer
to quiet, further from the static
of this world—this mind.

This evening, I see that it is not
what I look at that matters
but the closeness
of the looking. Which makes me think

of that fifth-grade boy
who, despite every reason
not to, smiled a smile that
held no trace of storms
or befores.

Whatever the reason, the holiness
of this ordinary evening fills me
until my insides ache. I stand still

in the middle of the darkening trail
and throw myself open, tucking
away the knowing that I'm always
one awake breath away from this thing
I've been living for.

Tuesday morning exhale

What if it's my job to sit here on this Tuesday morning
moving black pen across white
paper, listening to crows
cawcawcaw, and—now and then
the softest hint of birdsong. Deck he built
with his own strong hands holds
the weight of me, dog stretched
out on the not-quite-green grass, oaks
looking holy and brave and not-trying
and important and so damn patient—as always.

In the space between too much worrying
and thinking I should be doing
the dozens of things on my mental should-do
list, which is really more theirs
than mine, I swear I smell the ocean
in today's crisp, leaf-falling
air, which seems impossible
since the Pacific is 53.9 miles
from where I sit. But still—

I'm sure
I smell it. And it speaks
too. It says—

Shhh, quiet down, let belly breathe soft. It is good to be
here.

It is good to let go of the doing
that isn't yours to do. The being that's not yours
to be. It's good to breathe
and listen while you're still here to breathe and listen
to keep letting words find you
because, really—
you have to.

Lifting face to the kind
sun, I let myself exhale, an exhale

that reaches that ancient
knot in the center of my chest, and keep
my hand moving, humming thank yous
to the rhythm of the sea
that now I'm sure
I hear.

practicing

Today, I will practice noticing. Pretty patch of pink parting
winter sky, moss peeking through cracks
in the old sidewalk, how sadness calls me closer
to the unseeable, closer to my own tired
heart. And yours.

Today I will practice meeting my own longing until
the quietest voice becomes
the only one I hear. *Rest*, it whispers—unwind, unfold,
unfurl, unravel a lifetime of tired tangles. Strike a match,
light a candle, let the hard melt

into a slow stream of softness. Soft like petal, like
promise, like slow-drifting cloud. Notice
how the quietest voice holds you, how it throws
its sunshine arms around you and whispers:

*Hello Beloved, welcome. Welcome here. Welcome
home.*

while it's still here

It could be the story you read
this morning over coffee, about
the woman, exactly your age, who died
yesterday in a car accident

or the giant limb that fell
from the oak in last night's winter
storm. Or perhaps the memory

of how her tiny hands made
bouquets of dandelions
and then, together, you blew wishes
into the wind. Or maybe
the pausing for long enough
to notice lines etched deeper
into eyes one year older. It doesn't matter

what it is that makes you remember
that it's all temporary, that we don't
get to know when any
of it will leave. A remembering

that fills you with the deepest
kind of want to love every
miracle bit of it
while it's still here.

her prayer

Please, she prays, let me stop leaving, let
the holding be more important
than the hurry, the listening more important
than the lists, let me be

here

awake and new
for this quickly passing life.

message from a moment

Return, whispers the moment. I am right here.

Here in the rise and fall of breath, here
in the river of light and dark, dark and light
that runs through me, through you—
through sky and tree and early morning birdsong.

Bow in gratitude, whispers closed door, discomfort,
disaster, disappointment, let it all burn to the ground
so you can see, so finally you can see the moon
that lights your true—your truest way.

Let it be easy, whispers words on the page.

The wonder, the beauty,
the wildfire blossoms, are here,

and here

and here.

Return, whispers the moment.

Stop the struggle, the hiding, the steering, the seeking—
and be still. Be still until moon lights
your true—your truest, bluest,
most wondrously-you way.

the quiet teacher

I breathe better here.

Here where sand meets sea,
meets sky, meets setting sun. Here where I am released
from the burden of trying.

What seemed so convincingly worthy
of worry yesterday
sifts like warm sand through open hand.

The quiet teacher inside and all around,
invites me to hush. Invites you too. To hush everything
that is somewhere else, everything
that is anywhere other than
here.

This is your life, she whispers, cup it
in your warming hands. Let the warm seep into
what is numb, knotted, frozen, afraid.

Know that every bit of it is God breathing
all over you. And I don't mean the fist in the sky
kind of God. I don't mean the God with small,
stern, squeezing arms. I mean God whose arms are less
like arms
and more like wings. More like sun or song—

the quiet teacher who warms and grows
and lifts, who invites the whole worried
world to hush, to sing—
to wake. To wake.

the slow and simple

With the so-much going on in the world,
it is the slow and simple
that are saving me. Soft scent of sunlight
tucked inside fresh mint, sprinkle of cinnamon
on warm, buttered toast,
robin splashing herself clean and happy
in backyard birdbath.

On this Sunday morning, I choose
to set down the chaos,
the cravings—to pluck poetry and plenty
from pain, to settle into

the soft hum of now

where wanting and worry
used to be.

are you awake?

If you have not
seen beauty today
you are not looking. Eyes are open.
Legs move. Yet

you yawn your way
through another assumed
day. You pray for something
different, curse rain

for falling, shoo away
what you decide
is wrong. You throw open
every window
and look out and out
and out.

Please stop
the mindless doing
and come close.

Do you hear it?

Rest your hand
on your humming heart.

Do you feel it?

Feet rooted to ground. Fire
that never stops
burning. The slow drip
of honey.

Please stop and remember
that every unlikely bit of it
is laced in sunlight, all
of it quietly conspiring
to turn you toward true, toward you.

The kettle is whistling—
are you awake?

what silence said

This is what silence said to me today:

Trust what you can't see. Move forward
despite the wobbly groundlessness
of *I don't know*. Breathe, love, create, show up
as you are, everyday—*no matter what*. Go
to where wild irises grow. Say thank you
for all of it, weeds
cracks, sunbeams, that hand on your shoulder—
the forever throb of ache

it's all
a doorway, a hand leading you back
to grace.

busting down walls

I know this too shall pass
but, for just this one moment, every
single bit of me is singing. Unexpected
snowflakes fall from new morning
sky, music she makes
with her own growing hands
fills every room. Cup
of coffee, warm house—a bite
of the juiciest orange.

In celebration of this
color-filled moment, I can't help but
bust out some wildly ridiculous
dance moves. And then, right there
in the ordinary kitchen, all parts of me
are filled with a longing
to share this song—to wrap up

this extraordinary beauty
and deliver it like seed to every
hurting heart, to those who are hungry
or stuck or sad or sick, to those who feel
unseen or wronged or left out
or less than—for whatever reason.

Yesterday, I saw a single blooming daffodil.
Have you ever really
seen one? This work of art
could have only been made from artist
hands—like we all were.

I know this too shall pass, but for just
this one moment, let's join
hands and bust out some wildly
ridiculous dance moves. And please—

let us not stop. Let us never
stop seeing the art, the song,
the perfect poetic precision
in all of it.

step out into the sunshine

Take a break from the boring chatter
of your bossy little mind and step
out into the sunshine. There will be a breeze waiting
for you there, let it carry

the stuck, the stranded, the stagnant
away. And then, be *still*.

Be still until your remember the impossible foreverness
of sky, until you notice how ground holds
you steady no matter how stubborn the storm. Let

the whisper of the wordless speak
until it runs out of things to say.

Then sit and listen some more.

the space between

It does not matter what you call it
whether you name her a he
or a she, whether you imagine her
with two legs or four, branches
or wings. Or even if you don't believe.

It does not matter whether you enter
stained glass building
or kneel with forehead to dusty knees,
whether you hold hand out to receive
piece of bread or drop of sky.

It matters that, every day, no matter
how busy or old or mad or sick or
deep-in-your-bones-tired or unworthy you feel,
you stop long enough to listen to dove
say her early morning prayers,
that you rest inside the space,

this space

between thought and breath, before and next—
that you notice
that, with no help from you, sun
still blazes, body still breathes.

It matters that you listen until you see
that you are not the storm
that throws you violently to your knees

but the beloved, badass ocean
who holds and holds, who forever holds you
and every last, wildly inconceivable thing.

here

I am here with oaks, fern,
pine needled ground, here
with birds who sing for no reason, no matter
who is listening, no matter what day
or time it is. I wonder—

do they know how pretty they sound?

I am here distant from demands,
doubt, dirty floors, overflowing
drawers of indecision.

Here I no longer care
what you think of me. No longer wonder
whether I count. Here I almost fall in love
with not knowing, never
heard of the word *should*
or *try* or *tomorrow.*

I am bigness finally
found, no longer looking
for anything. Bigness who doesn't need
to be told because she
knows, who no longer
tries to be because she
is, has always been.

recipe for falling in love

The truth is
if we slowed down
and got close enough
we wouldn't be able to handle
the beauty

on this summer evening, everywhere
my eyes fall another miracle
stares back

giant oaks spread out like gods
big-eared bunnies munching under open sky
blackberries plump on the vine
invite me to taste their almost-sweet
insides. As I round the corner
I lock eyes with three deer—all of us still
and staring. With our eyes
we say—*I love you*. Winged ones
I cannot see sing
their end-of-the-day lullaby

each step lifts me higher
until at last, breathing more deeply
than I have in a long time, I see

the whole wide sweeping
tree-filled valley. And then—I weep
for, truly, I cannot handle the beauty
even from this distance. Then,
I would not make this up, a whole family
of wild turkeys cross the trail in front
of me—each one pausing
to wait for the next. All this

my heart gets to see, to feel—
to memorize. With light
now fading
I begin my long, slow
walk home, slow enough to notice
golden grass bent in prayer,
slow enough to bend too, praying
I will never stop
seeing

praying that I will walk
slow enough to fall in love
again and again
and again

even if it makes me weep
even it feels too much to handle

praying that each step
draws me close and closer still

all in one day

It starts with sunshine, cup of coffee warming
cold hands, a slow, breathing stroll
with the always-friendly trees, a love note
from a stranger.

And then, later, daughter weighted
from the hard of this living, pleading prayers
to a God it took me so long
to believe in, voice on the other end that says
the words your ears can't hear—
accident, didn't make it, I'm sorry.

The strike of the match that lights
the candle, whistle from the orange kettle—
the pouring, the steam, the drip of honey,
the first warming sip.

Sunshine. Reverence. Heartache.
Unthinkable despair.

All
in one day.

Life.

a prayer for every day

Let me breathe only grace today, only
that which slows, steadies,
softens, sparks

only that which points
to the blossoms inside the broken,
the poetry inside the pain, the nourishing
newness inside the now.

Let me breathe only grace
today, only that which invites
me to speak my very own
language for as long as I have breath,
only that which hums:

You can.
You will.

Let me breathe only grace
today, only that which notices the tired
and says, lie back, Love—rest
for as long as you need to. It's not
about how much you do
but how full you are.

And, my God, how beautiful you are when you are full.

today's question

As I watch the orange leaves let go
of the newly planted maple, the question arises—

what if I give myself completely to this,
to this that—*is*. To breathing, to breathing in coffee
brewed fresh and strong,

to this candle-lit house on this gray
November morning. Empty refrigerator,
dusty wood floors, fairy lights casting their warm,
sure glow. This house. The first
that I have named home. A home I
chose and keep choosing.

What if I give myself completely to the hard,
the scared, the sorrowful, the soothing—to the sound
of rain falling carelessly free, making its voice
heard. Which is what we all want,
isn't it? To be heard. To be free.

What if I give myself completely to the shake
of not knowing, to the knowing too,
to the often too loud of this sometimes
lifeless life. What if, completely, I give myself

to every thing, to the everything of being alive.

the cure for it all

Go gently today, don't hurry
or think about the next thing. Walk
with the quiet trees, can you believe
how brave they are—how kind? Model your life
after theirs. Blow kisses
at yourself in the mirror

especially when
you think you've messed up. Forgive
yourself for not meeting your unreasonable
expectations.

Praise fresh air
clean water, good dogs. Spin
something from joy. Open
a window, even if
it's cold outside. Sit. Close
your eyes. Breathe. Allow

the river of it all to pulse
through eyelashes
fingertips, bare toes. Breathe in
breathe out. Breathe until

you feel your bigness,
until the sun rises in your veins.

Breathe until you stop needing anything to be different.

life always knows

I rarely use words like glorious and sublime
but this circle of sunshine on this winter day
makes me want to skip

each curve in the trail greets me
like an old friend. Hard shadows
that have followed for days carry me now
to this soft clearing where crows
dip and glide to the hum
of something

they seem to hear inside me. The flap
of their wings reminds me that dark and light
need each other—invites me to stretch
arms wider, to stop making any
of it wrong.

Trust, the ground says
let the shadows be your compass, the poetry
that points to the other side

trust that life always, always knows.

it may not be convenient

to take the detour, the
I-don't-know-where-I'm-going
wandering way. To stand a little longer
in sun-soaked arms even if they
have to wait.

It may not be convenient to press pause on a life
going wildly too fast—to go back if you've taken too
many steps forward, to drink a cold glass of water slowly—
just because.

Don't let them hurry you. It is your pace you must find.

It's okay if you're late because you need
to scribble down a few more words, sing *hallelujah*
with the seabirds, hold her hand just a little bit longer.

Let them wait.

Maybe today is the day you'll light the candle, open
the good bottle of wine, write love letters in the sand
even though the tide will come and wash them away.

Maybe today is the day you'll see
that life
is conveniently right here.

i n

This breath invites you to write
the first word of your new story.
Your new story begins with this:

You matter.

before the forgetting

Come with me please, to a place before
the forgetting, when the bowl
was more full than empty, more whole
than cracked. To that place before
beyond beneath the terrible lie
of—*something's missing*. When all
of you, all of you was allowed.

Do you remember that place? The place before
you started to re-arrange, discard, demolish. Before
you began to quiet, cover,
smother, to seal tight the shaky
shutters—before you worried
about who was watching.

Do you remember who you were before
you thought it was someone else's
job to love the hurt away?

Come with me please, to a place where you
become the comforter of your own discomfort,
where courage tumbles out of you
into me, where breath softens, stretches,
deepens, dances—dances to the sound of true.

Imagine with me please, that we crush the crunch
of comparison, bend back the bolted
bars, smash through the stories, the walls,
the ceilings.

Can you see it? Bowl that never
empties, arms that forget how to close, you
wildly, wondrously, unquestionably full—gravity
pulling you closer, closer to whole. *Imagine.*

a long overdue apology

Dear Heart,

I'm sorry. I am sorry for dismissing you, dissing you,
doubting and degrading you, for not giving

you space to stretch out and breathe—
for trying to tidy you up, quiet
you down, stuff you into places
you never fit. I am sorry I have carelessly
and continuously cursed the skin and bones and stories
that have so faithfully held you.

Dear Heart, I am sorry for insisting that you
be more, feel less. For forcing you to shake off
the sorrow rather than scooting in close
while she shares her strange and sacred secrets.

Beloved Heart, I vow to put my ear
close, close to the pulse of you, to listen
for as long as you need me to. I promise to give you pen
and paper, to give you as much space
as you need to say your truest things.

Because I know, I finally, fully
know that everything
depends on it.

Quiet, courageous Heart, no matter what the world says
or does not say, please remember to let yourself need
what you need, feel what you feel. To, one slow spoonful
at a time, sip the nectar that brings you to life.

Dear Heart. I am sorry I haven't loved you better.

Let's begin again—perhaps with a nap, then
a hot cup of tea. Let us begin with pen, paper, a promise
to curl in close and listen until you exhale
your next truest thing.

Because I know, I finally, fully know
that everything, every last thing
depends on it.

the most important thing

I am making a home inside myself. A shelter
of kindness where everything
is forgiven, everything allowed—a quiet patch
of sunlight to stretch out without hurry,
where all that has been banished and buried
is welcomed, spoken, listened to—released.

A fiercely friendly place I can claim as my very own.

I am throwing arms open
to the whole of myself—especially the fearful,
fault-finding, falling apart, unfinished parts, knowing
every seed and weed, every drop
of rain, has made the soil richer.

I will light a candle, pour a hot cup of tea, gather
around the warmth of my own blazing fire. I will howl
if I want to, knowing this flame can burn through
any perceived problem, any prescribed perfectionism,
any lying limitation, every heavy thing.

I am making a home inside myself
where grace blooms in grand and glorious
abundance, a shelter of kindness that grows
all the truest things.

I whisper *hallelujah* to the friendly
sky. Watch now as I burst into blossom.

choosing me

I almost didn't come here today,
almost chose the list over the listening.

But here I am, breath full
of sunshine and salty sea. Softer, slower,
more wildly awake.

More of the me
I'm ready to be.

saving grace

When you're pressed up against
not enough and too much, when breath fades
to shallow, lifeless whimper and heart pulses
to a rhythm not your own, when you've walked into
something you are sure is bigger than you, try this—

stay.

Stay like trees stay when wind howls.

Breathe it in. The ache, the sadness,
the grief you are sure
will kill you—the joy you're afraid
will go away too soon.

Don't run. Or hide.

This thing in you is speaking, asking you
to listen. Let the bigness of this living land
right there inside of you.

Get on your knees and bow
to all of it. Watch, listen, marvel
at how grace comes in and holds you
for as long as you're willing
to be held.

already answered

She keeps looking for it
as though it is a lost thing to find,
as though there is a secret she has not yet been told,
as though if she tries harder, moves faster,
becomes more, she will catch it, finally.

She prays for courage, abundance,
love. She prays that someone
will see her, finally.

But the geese tonight, in all their musical glory,
remind her that it was never lost,
that it has always been tucked inside
each song-saturated moment.

And that every prayer
ever asked has already
been answered.

the river

Pay attention to what opens
and closes you, to what grows
you hard, melts you soft

these are the maps you've been looking
for, maps made of water
rock, breath, fire. If you open

all the way up, let every drop
of it enter and leave, enter
and leave, you will find yourself
floating in a pool of sunshine

like that time you held on to
nothing and the river caught you
in her quiet arms
and, for once, the trying
stopped.

This is what happens
when you let it all enter
and leave, the river
catches you in her quiet
arms and finally—
you float.

her song

Before she died, the tiny black bird

in my garden bed let me
touch her soft, fading feathers. In my gentlest voice,

I whispered: *I love you—*
because I did. I do.

I hope that when she sang her song
she didn't hold a thing back,
that her wild, wondrous wings flew her
just where she longed to go.

I hope her short life was a good one,
that when she took her last brave breath she felt

nested, nestled, safe, loved.

This is my wish for each of us, that we hold nothing back,
that we fly just where we long to go,
that we crack hearts open
by being exactly, precisely, entirely
who we are.

breathe yourself new

Maybe today is the day
to tip it all upside down, to shake out
what is stale and small and suffocatingly too sure

maybe today, rather than being tossed about
by enough-will-never-be-enough
expectations, rather than grabbing
for another word, another way, another now—
you could step outside and watch sky
make a new day. Maybe today

is the day to let go
of doubt's smothering hand, to stop hunting
for worthiness, to choose to follow only
what feels like tail-wagging enthusiasm, like firefly's
warm, sure glow. Like love sprouting roots
from the bottom of bare feet.

Maybe today is the day to remember
that if it doesn't grow the flame
warmer, truer, brighter, if it doesn't
feel like a deep dive into this boundless
breath of now, it's not meant for you

then lean close in
to your own glorious glow
and breathe yourself new

possibility

What could this life be
if you stop pretending
to be small when there are
rivers and skies
and field after sunlit field
of wildflowers
blooming inside you.

If, instead of looking for home
in every little thing, you get still
for a while and count
blessings—ladybugs
moonlight, smiles, tree
that shelters you

from rain and storm
and sometimes sunshine
too. Never once has she tried
to be something other
than a tree. Have you
noticed? Place your hands

on her quiet roots and listen
until you know what she
knows, then stay
and listen some more.

And there's the heart
that beats and pumps blood
to all the places it needs to go. And,
oh my gosh, how sometimes
you're sure it will burn a hole
through your chest
with how much it feels.

What could this life be if you decide
to tell the truth, if you let
your wild, true blue-ness splash
all over everything. Maybe
you would leave a puddle of sunshine
wherever you go.

What if you choose to believe
only thoughts that keep
you awake and in love, that
remind you

to stand up straight, to
throw on your cape. To be
the wildflower
you came here to be.

she decides

Today she decides to cross every last thing
off the list and adds only things
that bring her to life.

Things like:

Dance in the kitchen to the music
you used to dance to when you were young
and wore sexy the way only you could. Things like:

Take a long walk with the quiet trees,
inviting only open sky, birds' sweet song
and poetry to join you.

Today she decides that even though
there are wrinkles and gray and tired
stitched deep in her skin, and the world
tells her she is no spring chicken—

that she will choose young, that she will
pick up sexy again
and wear it the way only she
can.

Today she decides
that she is most certainly not chicken
but she will forever and always be spring.

komera

It is a brave thing to step on to the field, into
the arena—to each day, turn toward
blank page, empty canvas, to choose

to meet this beautiful, broken
world all over again. To sit inside
the mess, the mayhem, the—
I don't know.

It's a brave thing to rise up when you've hit
the ground hard, to sit still when fear
wants you to pick it up, pin it down—

to let dust settle
instead of hurrying
to wipe it clean.

It is a brave thing to forget the filters, to forgive
the unforgivable, to let hurt
be the hand that heals, to breathe,
to breathe until you feel your bigness.

To soften.
To open.
To listen.

In Rwanda the word *komera* means:
Be strong, have courage.

In the middle of the mess,
the mayhem, the—
I don't know,

it is a brave thing to slip off each
story of smallness, to let hurt be the hand
that heals, to take the next true step—
even when, even when, *even when*.

a message from love (part II)

Maybe, rather than grabbing for,
chasing after, pushing it out before
its time—you might step kindly closer,
turn courageously toward. Like monarch

resting her tired wings, like river
singing her way, carrying her song to sea,
might you hurry less, flow more—

might you be firm and fierce in your knowings.

Stars have never once asked
for permission. Have you noticed how surely
they guide, how unshakably they shine?

unbecoming

This morning, I sit inside the sorrow,
inside the circling-hawk worry that insists
I am doing it wrong, inside

the sunlight that meets me warmly
at the kitchen table, reminding me to breathe,
to accompany this pen on a long,
wandering walk, to stop asking to know
what comes next, to remember
that wobbly seems to be the way of things.

A sliver of a moment where all
of it is allowed—when I stop
trying to glue together

what was always meant
to fall apart.

a slow unfolding

I know it's not easy when you are stuffed full
of ocean, mountain, sunlight—when
there are infinite unwritten stories
that have been trying, for longer
than you can remember, to claw
their way out. When there is so, so much
you don't understand.

I know it feels impossible to keep trusting
when noise keeps growing noisier, when
it seems not one other sees
or believes, when the spark of trust
you have tried to have sometimes dims
to faint, faded flicker. When you are
just so, so tired.

But please, please Love, allow the noise
of this hustling world to roll, roll away
like a far-off distant wave.

Listen instead to the voice, the real voice, that sits
in the center of every
ancient thing. The voice that whispers:

*Please, please Love, be patient with you own, slow
unfolding.*

There is a rhythm, a readiness, a reason
you cannot see with your small,
impatient eyes. Keep coming *here*

to where words and heart gather,
where you can hear your own
voice speak. You will know it is your own
because she feels like ocean, like mountain,
like the kindest kind of thing. Like the slow,
fierce unfolding of a thousand sunlit wings.

a new way

Today, I see how all of it has needed to be
just as it was. I see how each
thing that seemed wrong was the moon
lighting a new way.

Today, I see how trying
to be good, trying to be enough
is more rubble in the way
of what has always been a well-lit path.

Today, I see that what matters most
can't be stolen or bought
or taken away—that no one but me
knows the way to a place only I can go. Sometimes

when I get real quiet
the moon tells me secrets only I
can hear. My only job is to lean back and rest
in her warm, strong arms until she shines me
a new way.

you are the ocean

Please, my god, *please*, do not
hold any of it back. Why
would you? It's like trying
to hold back the ocean
with the tip of your little finger.

This life, this force
this happy explosion that is *you*.

Come closer. Let wave
after wave tumble, let gust
after gust blow you entirely
to the ground.

Don't be afraid.

You are the ocean. Deep,
wild, fierce, infinitely bendable—
beyond compare. A thread of divinely
designed, intricately woven you-ness.

Not a thing can break you here
in your sweet hallelujah
depths. Not a single thing.

Let the hand that is whole reach for the one
that is broken. Stand up now. Spit out
the mountain.

Throw open your full moon wings.

what I've learned from the dark

It seems we must be stripped of the skin
of all we think beautiful before we open
to the kind of beauty that can't go away

it seems sky must pour and howl like it will never stop
before we notice the smile
of our own forever sun. It seems

we must hunt with starving,
hungry eyes before we know
this belly is and has always been
full. It seems this wall
deep in the center must be hammered down
before we let soft, breathing hands
curl in around us. Each drop

of dark carries with it a candle of holy
light—with each miracle breath
we are invited to turn toward
the nearest whispering spark
and, like mama bird
sheltering her baby, like pebble
in stream's safe lap

listen.

looking for home

Is there anything more beautiful
than to sit inside this here
holding pen and notebook
bare feet resting
on the kind, green ground
watching clouds hum
above this homesick world

Is there anything more
beautiful than to stop, to empty mind
of befores and afters—to listen
to the silent secrets
today holds, to hand over
the heavy
to bigger arms

Darling, one-of-a-kind
beloved, dying-to-be-free human
let your heart burst open wide
to this truth—

there is only one
you. There is only one
now. And—can you hear this? You are already
home.

Is there anything more beautiful?

your very own flavor of poetry

I keep forgetting that I am more,
more than this aging skin—these hips
these thighs, this belly
growing thicker. More than these calloused feet
that always, *always* insist I walk faster, farther
in some other direction. I keep forgetting that I'm more

than these scars made by my own
punishing hands, the ones you can see,
the others that run invisible through veins
and tired-of-trying inner parts.

I keep forgetting that I'm more than the voices
that scream *can't* and *never—right*
and *wrong*, more than this mind that oozes
indecision, this chest that squeezes
tight, that drops me hard in the shallow
and hollow of—*I don't know.*

I keep forgetting that I'm only a single breath away
from breaking free from these bars
I keep finding myself pressed beneath,
a quiet prayer away from remembering again
that I was put here to spit it all out
as prettily or un-prettily as it was and *is.*

On this dark, airless night the strong rock inside
begs to be remembered. Invites me
to repeat this verse until moon
smiles her pretty half-smile, until the winged one
wakes me with her new-day kiss.

You came here to hum the truth
that comes in only your color, to sit inside
the arms of a moment, to find breath in each drop
of dark, to skip and sip and frolic
with every fleeting firefly
of light.

You came here to give oxygen to words
to spin every stain and splash
into your very own flavor of poetry

You came here to look into your own eyes and whisper—
Beloved.

You did not come here to please, to perform,
to protect, to be better or to be liked.

You came here to feel the quake, the shake,
the thirst, the *love* deep in your rooted
center. And, head bowed, arms spread in surrendered
hallelujah!—crawl, skip, fly, tiptoe forward anyway
and no matter what.

Yes, for this you came

holy freedom

In the midst of chopping onions
and digging unnameable parts
out of the chicken carcass, before
I'm almost late getting my girls to soccer practice—

I scribble words, words that come
from nowhere, or from some mysterious
somewhere. Words that ask, no, *demand*,
to be written down

they are here in the shower as I reach, dripping,
for my notebook, here in the wanting kitchen when he
tells me about his day. Here

when I should be focused on driving
rather than taking dictation

I am a drunk driver swerving
from too many words, words that tumble
and spill and ask, no, *beg*, to be heard.

Thankyouthankyouthankyou
I say to God or whatever it is
that sends them

I pull over the first chance I get
so that I don't become one of
those people who kills
while intoxicated and write dizzily—
urgently. I don't care
that my hands smell like raw chicken, even this
is a metaphor for something. I'm sure.

After they all come out I exhale,
saying out loud to the wind

Thank you. Thank you. Thank you.

be still

The urge is to want
to *do* something, I know. Reach
for this, reach for that, check
it off, get it done. This living
has taught you that more
is better, that busy is boss.

Do more.
Go faster.
Try harder.

But, just for now, Love,
may I suggest you empty
your tired arms and

be still.

Listen to the rain. Light
a candle. Maybe watch
a cloud wander
quietly by. Be

the witness. The one
who sees the sky full of grace
that is always always always

right where your good feet
are planted.

the birds have all the secrets

Birds are singing their hearts out this morning. They sing
without a single note of self-consciousness,
never once asking for permission,
or worrying they are too loud,
or too soft, too young, too old, too off-key.

They wouldn't think to ask if now
is the right time or if their song
is as pretty as the others.

I sit here with daffodils and sunshine,
and listen. Marveling at the gush of grace
that can't help but come
when one is wildly, wonderfully,
wondrously who they are.

the poem that found me

How much is *too*?

Is 43 years too many to get it, finally,
to see that it's always been here,
this nameless something
that sits in quiet center, to trust
that this heart feels just what it came here to feel

I could call it love but it's so much more than that

for the man on the street whose eyes
blink sorrow, breathe hope
when I give just the littlest bit
of what I have. I can no longer
tell the difference between you
and me and I'm sure I want it to stay this way.

Too sensitive. Too emotional. Too dreamy. Unrealistic.

This morning while I run, soaked deep
in Oregon rain, breathing in, breathing out—
I wave arms in listening air
and belt out loud the words to that song
I can't keep from singing

I'm gonna celebrate and live my life

even though I don't know if there is someone
coming around that river-y bend. It feels glorious
to not care.

I love you.

Can I say these words too often
as I lean in close and closer
to these eyes—the ones that have forever looked
for *more*.

Is four decades too long
to try and grab hold of
what could never be held?

Breathing in. Breathing out.

Is there such thing as *too* if all of it leads
here, to this that wraps around,
permeates, saturates, satiates—
to this that is so much more than love.

There are wars going on while you write poetry.

I feel your heart like it's my own
and I don't want this to stop. Even if it means
I am on my knees more than sometimes.

Thank you poetry for quieting the war.

Until I can find more words
I'll keep breathing it in. breathing it out

I love you

because I do. Because when it comes to love
I am sure, there is no such thing as too.

learning to walk

I walk one step, then another
through holy golden light and all I can say
is *Oh. my. God.* Because there is no way anything
other than a divine, maker-of-miracles
could have made all this.

Wings swoop out of dried blackberry bush, trees give
and give and give, never asking
for a thing back. Single red leaf, rock pounded smooth
from wild sea. Eyes that look back.

All this, yet I hang my head, asking again and again
if there is God, purpose—reason. I ask
as I rush passed this undeniable holy.

Still, ground holds me. In every
moment, whether I stand or kneel
on bruised knees, whether awake
or asleep, whether I laugh
or weep—faithful ground
holds the *too too too* of me.

If all this doesn't call forth the treasures
I don't know what will.

Then, a gust rises from
that buried-deep place
and says:

How about this, how about you
toss the holy around as if there is no
end, no way, no lack—no empty. Because
there just isn't. How about you stop trying
to squeeze this holy inside words or
reasons.

Just lift your head, my love, and walk.

closer to free

It does not matter if it is good,
if you use the right words, or the prettiest
words, if you craft sentences complete
with commas and metaphors all in the right place.

It matters that it *feels* good, that you splash
around with joy, that you forget the world
for more than a while, that you make a merry mess,
feel the flap of wings against ribcage, that you mix
yellow and blue to make the just-right shade
of green, the green that reminds you of the field you
rested in

when you were still considered young.

It does not matter if you win the contests,
collect the rewards, the credentials,
the most pats on the back, if all your As
are straight, if all your sentences come to a full stop.

It matters that you forget the push
of performance while you lean in close
to opening crocus, that you let something
in you open too.

It matters that you drape words
off the page, miles off the page
even, that you write your way to true,
that you feel the shake of a voice finally found—

the flutter of a voice finally free.

could it be?

Could it be that today is the day you see
you have always had, always been
way more than plenty, more
than what covers you, more than eyes
that only sometimes see.

Could it be, perhaps, that today is the day
you fill every pocket with courage,
call yourself *sweetheart* for no reason, hold hands

with the parts of you that haven't yet
learned to breathe.

Could it be that today is the day
you follow your pen on a slow
stroll to somewhere,
each word a kiss—

a becoming, an unbecoming, your own hand
leading you closer, gratefully closer
to plenty.

she will not be quiet

will not water down words so you
can be more comfortable. She will not

let you dim the fire
from her eyes, the tiger
from her blood.

She is flower born wild
high note hit just
right, thirsty soldier dying
to come home.

She will no longer tiptoe so you can continue to sleep.

You will find her
here, moving winged hips
and bare feet, roaring
to the rhythm of her own firelight—

her ashes our medicine
guiding you here
guiding you home.

this too

Yes, this too is here for
you. Fly you cannot swat away, decades of dirt
beneath fingernails, argument
that boils blood, doors that slam shut,
doors that refuse to open. A longing
for an arrival in the middle of the—*not yet*. Yes, this too

is here for you, this moment and the last
and each dark, dull, dumb, seemingly
meaningless one in between—

gracious ground that keeps holding you even
as your body shakes
with grief. The shake. The ground. The
grief. Yes, even this. All of it a current pulling

you closer, closer to what will empty
the lying places, fill the blank
spaces . A real kind of filling. Not the fake kind.

Lazy afternoon when all doing is set
aside and you have only to feel sunlight warming
you from the outside in. Singing sparrow reminding
you of the song you still must sing. Silent sky speaks too—

don't swallow the ache, it whispers, hold her hand
instead, let her lead you to the next fertile step.

Tree that continues to blossom even
after storm has thrown her to the ground—she too
is your teacher. She too belongs.

The wobbly, wild, inconvenient mess
of it all when you can not
find the key, the door, the reason. Downpour
that drenches, cleanses, washes the dirt
away. Yes. This too, this too. *This. Too.*

this thing in you

will not take no for an answer.

This that somehow
shines strong
beneath the heavy hard hurry
of your conveniently
noisy life. This shapeless

something that shows up
everywhere—even when
you forget to notice.

It does not understand safe
or sensible, will not let you
get away with half-hearted
lifeless lies.

It's that wordless
something
that does not know how
to be quiet. It will continue knocking
until you throw open
the door. Until you become

Ablaze. Awake. Madly in love.

The dazzling artist
of your own
wild life.

everything is speaking

If you get quiet enough,
you will hear that every thing
is speaking.

Set me down, whispers mountain—
I was never meant to be carried. Lean every ruined
and ravaged bit of you against me, notice
how held you are.

You are not alone.

Forest with all its scorched
and fallen trees says—sweetheart, it's alright, it is
all right. Sometimes the mess has to be burned to the
ground to let the grand and glorious grow.

Let it burn.

Giant cottonwood calls—come, rest in the shelter
of my arms, hear these words—

You are a wonder.

Whatever terrible thing
has happened to you does not
need to keep happening. You
are worlds stronger than your wounds.

A pause in the middle of the day says—remember,
remember darling, you are not
the broken bits in the burn pile
but the one who sees
the wreckage and says—

I am still here.

If you get quiet enough
you will hear that every thing
is speaking.

Set it down. Let it burn.

Write the first word of your new
story. Make it your very own.

holy liberation

I will declare it out loud—decidedly,
mightily, quietly, steadily, with the kind of fire
that burns through all but the truest things.

I will howl it to the wild, midnight
moon. I will say it silently
to the darkest part of night.

I
am
enough.

I will gather up the flame, the fury,
every fear and fallen warrior, the tiny, afraid,
trying-to-be-good girl who kept getting knocked down
and forgot only her own legs could lift her back up.

I will whisper to her in the night:
You are a warrior. Look at how far
you've come. You never
needed to be anything other.

I will tell her, over and over
again that I am ready to be, that I will forever
be her greatest believer. I will promise
her with my pinky.

With a fierceness only liberation can muster, I will hush
each voice that makes me feel anything less than
beautiful.

I will declare, claim, reclaim
as many times as it take:

I
am
enough.

With a roar that quakes and shakes
the whole sleeping world awake,
I will stake my flag to the ground.

I will be a soldier for my own rising heart.

It will be the most epic
homecoming ever.

her new story

She is rising. She is rising up and out
of the stuckness of her yesterdays.

She will slip off the cloak of smallness
and drape, adorn, bless and blanket herself
in her own brand of bigness.

She will surrender the suffocating squeeze
of conformity, the dizzying race to nowhere,
she will stop waiting for someone else's hand
to show her the way only she, only she
can know. She will stop waiting. Period.

She will remember that all
she has been chasing
rests, rests *here*, here where feet
kiss fertile ground, here where body
beats and breathes
and breathes
and breathes.

She will have the audacity to take up space,
to follow the trail of her own wild longings,
to be herself, all of herself. Only herself.

She will invite you to join her.

She is rising. She is rising up and out and through
the door that has always been hers
to open. She will remember and remember again
that she belongs. That she belongs to herself.
She will remember that she is necessary.

She will insist, she will persist,
she will not take no for an answer. She will be her own
savior, her own superhero, her own guide,
her own guru. With the help
of her sisters, of course.

She will follow her own rhythms,
her own reasons, she will slip into
the new, the never before. She will plant
herself firmly and decidedly
in her own certain skin.

She will bow to the crooked, winding ways
that led her from there to here. She will bow to each
of her sisters, to all women and girls, to all beings
everywhere. She will promise to hold
her own hand forever. She will promise
to hold yours too.

She will listen to the wisdom of rivers
and wildflowers, to the great, growling hunger
deep, deep in her belly. She will listen
to the silent places between, between
then and now, between there
and here, between this word
and the next. She will write
a new story, a story
that begins and ends
with love.

She is rising. She is rising up and out
of the stuckness of her yesterdays.

Dear Sisters, do you hear her? Come, she calls,
let us say each other's names,
let us reimagine, let us gather,
grow, build, become, let us become
the roaring wildfire
that burns, that burns the small away—

let us rise, let us rise
together. Together
let us rise.

love

Stop asking: *Am I good enough?*

Ask only: *Am I showing up with love?*

staying in love

From my hiding place in the sunlight, I watch
the neighbor with his old, graying dog. Side-by-side,
one slow step after another, they walk.

I watch as the man pauses, bends down
and close—holds her soft, big head
in his two gentle hands.

They do not know I am watching,
that my insides must stretch
to make space for this aching breath
of tenderness.

Have you listened to the winged ones today?
They are full, so very full of themselves. *It's a brand new
day!* they say. *Did you know that anything
is possible, that staying, that staying in love
is the cure for it all?*

I wonder—what if we pause more, allow
this fading breath of life to stretch us awake,
what if we make time to listen to our feathered
friends. To strangers too. To those who disagree.

Dear neighbor, whoever you are, whatever side you are
on, no matter how deep the disappointment, how
dreadful the despair, how wild the winds of worry, I invite
you to the table. I offer you a bowl of spilling sunshine, a
cup of splashing song. *Dear stranger*, whoever you are,
wherever you stand, let us take one slow, anything-is-
possible step closer, let us be the gentle hands that hold,
the wings that stretch—that stretch one another awake.

telling it true

Share a page of your story and I will
share a page of mine. And, please, let us not
leave out the terrible, tripping parts. Let us not share
what is plasticly polite and pretty
but what is undeniably, pricelessly true.

Please, no coating with sugar,
no pretending disguise. I want to see the real
beneath the *I'm fines*, to hear the enchanting everything
of your being, of this being alive.

I promise I will open the way sky
opens for stretched out wings, that I will listen
as if there is just this, just now—
just you.

Let us weave in space for slivers of silence, for slow,
seeing sips, for the true to seep in
and through, space to notice
peek of light through thick of gray.

Is there anything more beautiful
than this? Than you, than me? Than telling
it true, than opening—than listening?

stitched together

The meadow she visits most afternoons is now blooming
tiny white daisies, sky shines her clearest
most wondrous blue, cherry tree has gone ahead
and blossomed her prettiest pink. All this

while we are told to separate,
stay home, shelter in place. This
while last breaths are taken, while grievers
try to find a reason.

She stands still and breathes. She breathes
extra long and deep for those who can't.

She wonders if her heart is big enough
to hold this degree of beauty,
this degree of grief.

She closes eyes and sees arms stretching
around the globe, each heart beating
in rhythm with the other. A colorful quilt of comfort

wrapped and woven, stitched
with suffering and song,
and song and song.

life's storms

I want to save them all. Salmon splashing happy
a moment ago, now flopping in fisherman's empty
bucket, the one whose grieving
family leaves flowers on the side of the road—
the grieving family too. Those who are continually
thrashed by life's sure and steady storms.

I want to save them all, the now-wilting
dahlias we bought at the market last week,
the tired seekers who don't pause long enough
to notice their holy, passing
moments, those who see the finger pointing,
but never quite see the moon. Like me yesterday,

breathlessly running from one there
to another, leaving crumbs
of myself along the way. Yes,
I want to save her too. Most importantly,
most of all.

breathing my way back

I am in the kitchen peeling sweet potatoes,
chopping the onions she grew from her own
rich soil, gently squeezing one avocado
after another until I find the one
that is the perfect age of ripe.

Hands are busy peeling
and chopping, while mind
skips from one terror
to another—cars and houses drowning
in water, forests on fire, monster
winds that rip roofs off hearts
and homes. People running
from war to more war.

Fingers painted in soft, green
avocado now, feet stand
on the hickory floor, mind

chasing and trying
to outrun
the fire, the flood
of too much.

Then, I remember—
to *return*. To breathe
my way back
to where the body is.

I remember that instead of scrolling
and chasing and running, I can
roll out the yoga mat, I can
bow to every tree
that has ever stood. I can
feed myself so I can be
one of the ones who helps
rather than hurts.

For now, though, I am still here
in the kitchen, peeling sweet potatoes,
chopping onions, making a meal
so my family and I can sit gratefully
around the table and eat.

another Monday

It's Monday again and I don't want to. Don't want to drag
myself out of this warm, everything bed,
don't want to reenter the dizzying
disease of busy, the tight-lipped
expectations of *polite appropriate faster more.*

Don't want to read the terrible
headlines. Want to burrow deeper
beneath blankets, deeper into the quiet dark,
deeper into dreams that carry me
to a new world, a world I
get to make, free

from fighting, free from *ours* and *theirs,*
free from the chronic ache
of this too-short life.

I want to burrow deeper into the quiet
and dream dream dream,
dream a better place, a place

where love stays and stays,
where every single breath of a thing,
is included.

please, do not wander

I know the world looks lost, broken,
in too many pieces to repair, that *here*
might be the last place
you want to be. But please, please Love,
do not wander. Do not stray into
crowded streets, cowardly corners—

it is not possible to drink from what is empty.

From my kitchen window, I watch
two hummingbirds sip side by side. Yesterday
they chased each other away
chirping *mine mine mine*. Today, somehow,
despite the breathless weight of midwinter,
they have learned that there is plenty—
the tenderness of their sharing makes me cry.

As I watch them, I think, if tiny birds can learn to share,
to sip side by side, maybe
we can too. Maybe, despite the weight
of this deep, dark, relentlessly
draining winter, we too can learn
to drink from the fountain of plenty. To resolve to stay
and stay right where we are.

between you & me

As I bend down to water the echinacea blooming red
in our garden bed, the softest morning breeze
finds me. And then, the sweet scent of jasmine
mixes with the kindness of birdsong.

I sit here now, cup of coffee in favorite
ceramic mug, pen moving slowly across empty
page, best dog friend stretched out beside me.

Waves of gratitude roll in again and again—

thank you, I say to no one and every one,
for this moment when all of it hums
in healing harmony. When, for once, I forget
the rising numbers, the breathlessness,
the rampant infection of hate.

As I reach for the book I'm reading *Between the World
and Me*, a hummingbird hovers
within inches of my face

as if to demonstrate how to soften the space
between worlds—between you
and me.

better together

And we see that most of all, it is the little things.

Magnolia that bursts into blossom when no one
is looking, music that spills, pours, splashes from their
balconies to ours because maybe, perhaps—
we see that there's no such thing as mine.

And we see that most of all, it's the little things—

poetry sipped slowly, home-cooked meals
around kitchen table because, for today,
we are all here. Today there is time.

And we see that most of all, it's the little things—

a word, one after the other that comes through
me out to you—words like, *what do you need?*
How can I help? Words like, *I understand,*
we're in this together. Please, let's share.

And we see that most of all, it is the little things—

invitation to take a slow, deep breath,
a breath that brings you back and back and back
to here, to something greater deeper wider
than small ideas of what should be. An invitation to
remember
that, still, and especially now, together is the answer.

Always breath. Always here. Always better together.

birdsong

If you find your attention being pulled
by the sound of birdsong, let yourself
be pulled. And then, no matter how hurried
you think you are, stop
whatever you're doing

and *listen*.

Listen as if this moment is all there is,
as if every answer to every question you have ever asked
rests in the rhythm of inhale and exhale.

Listen as if one day you will run out of time to listen.

Listen until you are so full of song
you can't help but sprinkle it like seed to every
hungry heart. And when bird lifts her wings
to fly, go, please—

go fly with her.

God on the street corner

I can't stop thinking about them, homeless man
and his dog, side-by-side
on the street corner. The smile of—*I see you*
from his eyes and mine. The joining
of hands for a heartbeat or two. Gentle
laughter. The way he bent down low
to pet his dog. So much giving
and receiving in the rhythm
of that short song.

I've always wondered
about God.

Is there one? Does he have a purpose or a plan
for all this? Does she live in the heavens? Does his love
depend on how good we are? Or, perhaps—
is she or he too big to fit inside gender
or sky? Too full to discern or deny?

I don't know about any of this. I suspect these
things don't matter in the case of God.

I do know I saw her this afternoon, in that man's
smile, in the unlikely joining
of our two songs, in the sweet words
said as we waved goodbye.

And then—later, in the kitchen
when I rest my head
on his shoulder for a heartbeat
or two. A moment where we forget
about dinner and doing
and stay right where we are.

there's work to be done

The bad news keeps coming. With each image
and headline, I reach for another tissue.

How? How is there room in these small bodies? Surely
they are too small to hold it all.

But, somehow, they do.

We wake again to another new day, drink coffee,
pack lunches, go to work, fall asleep in the evening
with children tucked safe in their beds.

Thank you, we whisper to the night.

Each breath a prayer for the hurt and loss—
for the planet and people and animals
we want to save but can't.

Today, in between pacing
and clicking and crying, I light
a candle. I sit on the couch
with my very warmest blanket
and look out the window. I watch rain
and leaves fall from sky. I watch
two gray squirrels chase each other
up and down oak trees. I sip hot tea.

Later, I will stand in the kitchen I still have
and make homemade soup
and pumpkin bread.

It's okay, the quiet says—
*you are still here. Come now, jot down
a few words.*

Come now, there's work to be done.

Dear Child,

Listen. Rise from the tight walls of your troubled thinking.

Take your message of love,
of gentleness, of unity, and, please—
please speak it. Write it, paint it, dance it
sing it. Look up and smile

when another walks by. Toss love
around with the wildest abandon. Listen
to trees, sky, tomatoes that grow ripe
and red and brave and beautiful
out of the burn pile. Rise up.

Stop letting littleness win.

That nod of gentleness, of—
I. see. you. could mean everything. It could
mean one less bomb, one less
war, one less mother or child
or country on their knees.

Dear Child,

Put your weapons down.
Love fiercely.
Rise up—please.

Everything depends on it.

my kind of love

You will know her because, like sky
there is nowhere she is not. Because she sees through
what is banged up and blocked and bruised
and says—*tell me more*. Because she never

shrinks you with shame or needs you to be anything
less or more or other.

You'll know her because, like the sun, no matter
how hard you fall, her flame does not fade or falter
or flicker or flounder or ask for anything
back. And what you see as failing, she sees
as fresh fuel for the fire.

You'll know her because when you cannot see, she'll
take your shaking hand and do the seeing for you,
showing you how those blocks and bruises
are buds waiting to burst into blossom.

I am all yours, she'll remind you. *All yours.*

You'll know her because she never asks for more
but, rather, whispers softly:

Set it down, beloved—rest.

And, with her still and steady breath
singing sweetly inside you—finally, you will.

the question

Just for today, let's pretend
we don't have these bodies
skin, scars, bones—weathered fence
that keeps it all in.

Instead we would be here, one heart beating
to the rhythm of every thing. Mountain,
tree, rock, wild wind. Nothing in the way.

Do you hear it?

All of it is asking and asking
the same ancient question.

What is that thing stamped into
your bones—that thing that won't stop
calling your name?

There is a reason

and it is all
yours. Will you step toward
or away?

what can we do?

Get closer. Don't decide. Ask
questions, then listen
like a tree listens—

still and rooted in your brave.

Remember, what matters most
in this wounded world
can only be given, never
taken away—

never stop giving.

Open arms as wide
as they will open.
then open them some more—

Never stop opening.

Keep saying:

I hear you.
I see you.
I love you.

Don't leave anyone out, never
leave anyone out.

Watson

I'm pretty sure our new kitten thinks
our middle-aged dog is his mama.

At first, he hissed and made himself big
whenever he saw her, but now

he nestles into the warm curve
of her belly and purrs. He even
closes his eyes while she
licks him clean.

The other day, he helped himself
into the pantry, and, I swear, tried
to open the doggy jerky
for his new mama. After dinner

they chase balls and each other
around the house until
one of them has to lie down.

Two entirely different species
showing us what love looks like,

teaching us how to hiss
less, how to purr more.

like the wildflower

Precious little wildflower,
tell me your name. No—
never mind, tell me instead how you
hold so steady through seasons and storms,
how it is that the closer I get
to your silent center
the more I can feel my own.

You, with your five petals
made of the softest pink,
please whisper your secrets, please
show me how to be so completely,
how to say so much without even a word.

And you, seeker beside me,
don't tell me your name,
tell me what it is you can't stop
wanting, what it is that brings you
to your knees, makes you weep with something
so much bigger than joy.

I promise to listen like wildflower does,
to hold you until you come back
to that silent center,
until you come back, finally,

to love.

guru in disguise

There is something about the way
morning light rests on old, mossy oak
that quiets the loud in me, invites
me to set everything down.

As I step closer, I see
that she has wrinkled and grayed with age,
has weathered seasons, storms—indifference.

Still, she stands.

She is a resting place for gentle,
winged ones, a playground for frolicking gray
squirrel. A sharer of secrets to anyone who takes time to
listen. She is shelter for those who are worn.

Someday she will be gone,
will have turned into something else.

For now, though, she is here
sharing secrets, catching sunshine, inviting us
to turn toward the light
and listen.

the everything she gives

This deep breath of autumn reminds me
to say thank you. Reminds me to bow
with deepest reverence for the everything She
gives. And gives and gives.

Maples draped in gold, ground that holds each
drop of sunshine, each drip of rain.

I stop in the meadow and listen to singing birds,
watch squirrels spring from tree branch
to tree branch. Look a doe straight in the eye—
this is what courage looks like, I think.

Last night we ate homemade soup and bread
around the kitchen table. She gave us all of it. The soup,
the bread, the kitchen table too.

Acorns strike the ground with a startling
slap crack smack,
perhaps to shake us from seasons
and seasons of selfish slumber.

She is like that, always speaking, always
teaching, always giving it all away.
Urgently pleading:

Wake up. Pay attention. Give back before it is gone.

we were made for this

I want to fill this space
with words that will erase the distance
between your certainty and mine

make room under the big, empty sky
for grace to sit, move closer
until skin touches skin, eyes see eyes.

Maybe we can take a good, deep
breath, clear body and mind of all
that's come before. Promise
to pay attention, to stay—
especially when it hurts.

Maybe this time we will see
that it has nothing
to do with who we've been
or who we think we are

and everything
to do with being fiercely here—
like breath is for life. *Yes,*
like that.

Maybe—perhaps, we can begin
and begin again with—*I don't know.* See
that it takes just one step *toward*
to erase the distance
that was only ever a thought.

Dinner is on the stove, will you join me?

lessons from a
second grade classroom

When I set down the lesson plans
and begin to speak about kindness, they all
look up. Pencils lie still on desks, restless arms
and legs and mouths quiet now.

As I talk about how each of us
struggle with things others know
nothing about, about how kindness is the best
kind of medicine, the brown-eyed one
raises her hand and words tumble
out with a fierceness that has been blazing
for far longer than seven years.

My grandpa taught me about kindness
but he's dead now. Now I have to be mean
because I live with my grandma
and she's the meanest person I know.

Her words catch fire and burn right through
whatever hard things are in the way.

The children are quieter than they've been all day.

The one who was fighting at recess, stands up
and opens her arms to the brown-eyed
one—others, even the boys who
have been fidgeting uncomfortably
from the other side of the room, join them. The two
who hurt each other with words are now holding hands.

I watch them with a smile, children blazing
the way, not with pencils and worksheets, not
with straight lines or straight A's, but
with a kindness that burns
through whatever hard things
are in the way.

I pick up the lesson plans and toss
them into the recycling, vowing
to remember, to help them remember,
that this—is what matters most.

my plea

This body is too small
to hold it all, ancient
stories, yours and mine
deep, deep wells

of tangled ache. The light so very tired
of being pressed down, kept in
condensed.

Let's gather it up, this burning orb
of brightness, let it breathe, let it breathe
in our open palm. Until it warms away

the you, the me, the every thing—
until there is only wordless
river of calm, lulling, lulling us
awake

this letting go

Another autumn has arrived,
and with it everything is letting go.

Acorns announce themselves
with a startling smack, trees
that were dressed in orange red golden,
are now leafless, light—luminous. Fallen apples
fill the air with the scent of another season.

If we pay attention, slow
to the rhythm
of days growing shorter, darker,
we will see how it's done,
this letting go—

the sure way nature shows us
how easy it can be.

reunion

The moment bare feet
meet kind mat, there is
a certain kind of relief. Breath
deepens, mind quiets, every bit
of me steps into now. Like when
you enter the arms
of someone who loves you
more than anything.

Child's pose
Peaceful warrior
Downward Dog. A body
learning to love itself.

At the end of practice
we press one palm to the other
and say *Namaste*. And always, I think—
could there be a more perfect word? A word that means:

The light in me bows to the light in you.

Isn't this what the world
needs most? To see the light
in ourselves, each
other. To bow and bow
and bow to every
last thing.

what I really need

What I really need is a red, dusty road,
bare feet next to other bare feet, eyes that say—

I hear you. I see you. Me too.

Hands on shoulders, bodies walking
side-by-side. Each step
a thank you for what is real
and right and true.

What I really need is to feel, to really feel,
hot water pour from the tap, to allow
all the healing color—
reds, oranges, yellows, greens,
blues, to seep into the hard
and hollow, to lie down
and look up at the moon with your
eyes. To bow in gratitude, in awe,
for the profound goodness of such things.

What I really need is to meet
the other with doors thrown open,
to listen, to really listen
to his and her and their brave and beautiful story
like it's the only thing that matters. To offer
the kind of listening that does not measure,
to look the other in the eye and say—

I hear you. I see you. Me too.

What I really need is to drink a glass of water slowly,
because there is enough—there is enough fast
in this world. And every real thing
is found inside the soft arms
of a moment.

And because, in the midst of so much trauma
and terror, it is vital to bow to such holy, ordinary things.

What I really need is to get close enough
to notice tiny lines stitched in sad, smiling faces, to see,
to really see, that every dream and detour, every
disguised-dead-end has brought me to this, to this real
place—

where red, dusty road meets
bare feet and hearts, to this place as known and needed
as your inhale, my exhale. To this very real breath, the one
we can finally breathe together.

be that person

Please, be that person who says it anyway,
who begins despite the trembling, who—
despite every grumbling protest,
stays where you are.

Please, be that person
who sings with the crickets
who breathes breaths of gratitude
who knows, who *knows*
there is no thing
but love.

Please, don't stop
when you feel beaten, tired,
hopelessly lost, beyond repair—
wild with ache.

Please know that I will be here
to catch you, to carry you into the clearing,
to invite you to say—*yes yes yes*.

Please, be that person.

nothing extra

I wonder what's on the other side
of her smile, the carefully applied mascara,
the titles, the awards, the polite choice of words.

I wonder what was there before,
before the selfie, the filters, the snaps,
the chats—before she decided something
was missing.

I wonder if she's ever considered that likes
have nothing to do with love.

I wonder what she thinks about
in the moments before sleep, if she sees
that we all feel small in the same
human way, that each of us is reaching
for our own hope of home.

I wonder what would happen if she empties her hands,
steps into sunshine, bathes in the tiny sprinkles
of light, maybe leans against the oak for a while.

Just leans. Just listens. Just rests.

Perhaps she would see that she is beautiful before
the filters, with or without the likes,
stripped of the pretend, the made up, the make believe—

just resting here with nothing extra
like the lit up winter oak.

no such thing as other

It is a perfect evening for a walk. You
and the river by my side—trees,
birds, breath, sky
filling us with color and song.

As we walk by the old homeless
couple, sitting on the riverside
bench, the woman points to my sandals. With words
I almost can't hear, she says—*I like your shoes.*

Her smile reveals only a handful
of teeth, tiny rotting apples just about
to fall. The old man doesn't speak with words
but with a grin that splashes everything
warmer, lighter.

I want to know their story, want to know
how, even without beds or roofs or bank accounts
or titles or stylish new sandals,
they show us that *come as you are*
is the truest meaning of beautiful.

After we chat about the upcoming
weekend weather, she says,
Happy Mother's Day. Words that feel
more like *thank you* and—
we're in this together.

We walk away with bigger
hearts, doors swung open
to let the other in. Four people sharing
the same breath and sky, filled full
with something that feels like
the truest meaning of home.

I am still floating in their warmth, bowing
to every mile walked in their old,
tired shoes, thanking them for inviting us
to sit for a while by their fire, for reminding
us that there is no such thing
as other.

drunk on love

Let's get drunk on love, shall we?

Drunk on the knowing that this here,
this pulsing hum of now, is all
that matters.

Silent gray clouds, wide open
field where there is no
such thing as wrong. Hearts
that still beat, hearts that get
to beat.

Let's listen, shall we? To the breath
that invites us to land
with both feet on the ground of this sleepy
afternoon, to set down
the hangover of every staggering yesterday.

Together we will lead each other back
toward the truth we keep forgetting—
this truth:

Our Beloved is right here.

Here in the eyes that stare back,
here in the rich, organic soil
of our deepest ache, here
in the empty space before
the next life-giving inhale.

Come, let's sip slowly, or drink in deep,
wild gulps. This small, intoxicating sip
will give us everything if we let it—

let's let it, shall we?

don't wait

We pretend there will be a later,
a some-other-time to do the thing
our insides know
we must do. We wake one morning
to find the trees almost empty
did we see a single leaf fall?

We tell ourselves there we will be another time
to paint it, to write it, to sing it, to dance it, to be it—
that tomorrow will be a better day
to open wider, to hold closer, to say
I love you.

We fill our moments with more,
pull away just when our heart begins
to feel. We forget our insides hold the secrets
we've spent a tired eternity trying to find.

A woman I've never met but know I know
is dying. Last night in my dreams
she whispered with a timeless, gentle burning—

Hold longer, love deeper, let the good pour
out as if your life depends on it. Whatever you do—

don't wait.

a message from love

Open. Open every cracked and lonely
window, every false and frightened door.

Open clenched hand, closed mind. Let the tight,
the tense, the tangled, the untrue,
sift, sift slowly through.

Open like heron opens as she returns
to wind, unabashedly unfurling,
stretching, lifting, lifting her sunshine wings.

Open. Open to every weary traveler,
to those who have lost their way. Even when
you disagree. Even when
they are unkind, unpopular, unlikeable. Invite
them to tea. Listen. Listen
like you have never listened before. Marvel
at how alike you are, at how sweet the honey.

Unclench, unfold, unfurl,
un-decide. Pour it all
out. Take it all off.

Open like ground, like page opens to receive
fallen leaf, fallen words, like breath opens
to make space, to make space for more.

Open ten thousand times a day.

Rest and refill when you
need to. Then open,

open some more.

it could be

a smile or a poem. Or new day light
that finds you through open
window. Or, perhaps, remembering
that tomorrow was never promised.

It could be the scent
of baking bread, the first chill
of autumn that has you reaching
for your favorite wool sweater. Or maybe
it's the noticing of how easily
red maple becomes and lets go.

It could be taking today off
to be still, to un-know,
to notice. To practice loosening
your troubled grip
because grace can never
be gripped or grabbed.

It could be choosing
softness in a world grown hard
because you're tired of hurting
and being hurt and mercy
is the best kind of medicine.

It could be an invitation to gather
around the listening table
where every color is beautiful, where
there is no blame,
no shame, no them—no other.

It could be any of these things
or no thing at all, that remind you that, really,
only a few things matter—

Food. Trees. Words. Love. Mostly love.